Cool School

by Louise Franklin

NATIONAL GEOGRAPHIC LEARNING | CENGAGE

This is my school.

window

entrance

field

track

2

I learn the same things that you do.
I learn science, math, and history.

Is this a school?

director

bench

stage

Yes, it is. It is a school for actors.

Is this a school?
Yes, it is.

screen

simulator

6

windshield

gauges

It is a school for pilots. Students at
this school learn to fly airplanes.

Students at this school learn to fight wildfires.

airplane

parachute

hard hat

fire

parachute

They jump from airplanes to fight
fires on the ground.

What do students learn at this school?

monitor

mouse

keyboard

headphones

They learn to make video games.

This kitchen is a school for chefs.

garbage

sink

counter

pot

stove top

12

knife

plate

pan

The students learn to cook. Yum!

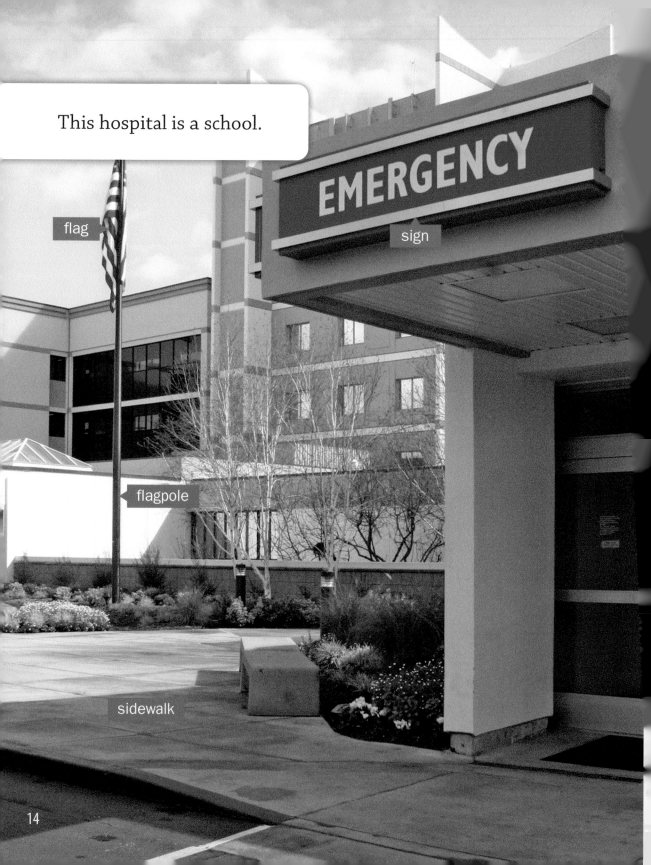

This hospital is a school.

flag

sign

flagpole

sidewalk

patient

notebook

The students help people who are sick.
They learn to be doctors.

There are many different schools.
What do you want to learn?

architecture

art

music

auto repair